MAMA

a poem by

Michelle Naka Pierce

Finishing Line Press
Georgetown, Kentucky

MAMA

Copyright © 2025 by Michelle Naka Pierce
ISBN 979-8-88838-958-4 First Edition
All rights reserved under International and Pan-American Copyright Conventions. No part of this book may be reproduced in any manner whatsoever without written permission from the publisher, except in the case of brief quotations embodied in critical articles and reviews.

ACKNOWLEDGMENTS

With gratitude—To Charmain Schuh for including *Moon Island Memorī* in the NOW exhibition at Naropa University's Cube Gallery (Spring 2025). To the editors of *Conceptions Southwest* XV.2 (Fall 1992), *The Paddock Review* (Spring 2025), and *FENCE*, Issue 43 (Winter 2025) for publishing excerpts from this chapbook. And to Leah Huete de Maines, Christen Kincaid, and everyone at Finishing Line Press for supporting *MAMA*.

Publisher: Leah Huete de Maines
Editor: Christen Kincaid
Cover Art: Michiko Masuda Pierce, circa 1948, age 20
Author Photo: Liana Martina Maneese
Cover Design: HR Hegnauer

Order online: www.finishinglinepress.com
also available on amazon.com

Author inquiries and mail orders:
Finishing Line Press
PO Box 1626
Georgetown, Kentucky 40324
USA

Every family has its own collection of stories, but not every family has someone to tell them.

—Lyn Hejinian

For Mama

Were you to glide—

You thought you were writing the body. But you did not understand it until now. And even so, its mysteries persist. The morning the bomb drops on Hiroshima, Mama is five hundred miles away. Same distance to your childhood home. Firestarter. The sound of a frequency that burns. The memory of homeland turns to ash in cognitive decline. Mama doesn't recall your first word. Doesn't know if it was in English or Japanese. The evaporation of language. The disintegration of gesture. You study kinesiology as a dancer. Skeleton muscles motion. But what of the small movements that begin in the brain unseen?

In the bath, Mama teaches you a children's song:

> Ame ame fure fure kaasan ga
> Janome de omukae ureshii na
> Pichi pichi chapu chapu ran ran ran

The ofuro rain. The tiny hand splash.

These days you sing to her as she falls asleep. Thunderstorms shake these walls holding our shallow voices. This score that accompanies the start of one life / the end of another.

Document a seam. Follow a stitch from Japan to the US. Identity travels as an immigrant might / on a two-week voyage in the Pacific Ocean. From Yokohama to San Francisco. Seasick and pregnant. And the only thing Mama can keep down are crackers and Coca-Cola. This invitation / to document / reverses the static notion of this text. This stitch. This is not an exercise, but a way to contribute to the function of space. In other words, identities travel the continuous frieze. That which is seen by spectators. The question of difference remains open in this call for dialogue. And you must participate in the recovery efforts.

Mama holds your hand and admires the softness of your skin, recalling that as a child she had chilblains.

She tells you the loneliness of no one speaking her language and you regret that you never learned.

I was fifteen, she said,
when my high school
used to help a factory
near the ocean.
An air-raid siren
compassed the city
and we headed underground
across the street.
Two or three times a day
B-29s hit Tokyo with
Napalm and missiles.
From the shelter door,
I watched
as the building we worked at
burned.
As my friends and I
walked home to Tsukishima,
I saw Ojiichan
racing toward us;
he was carrying a shovel.

You clench her hand as if she were slipping.
No mama.

Anata no hada wa zutto yawarakai desu.
Your skin is much softer.

Only these are not her exact words.

You've been writing her story for over thirty years. This failure of syllables and memories and languages and more. Retrograde comparisons. In her tenor, there is isolation. In your isolation, there is remorse.

There is a moment when language transcends this physical form. *A poet is the words she embodies.* You repeat this sentence, hoping for divine intervention from this colonialized / assimilated life. The horror of looking in the mirror and being betrayed by what you see. All this and not resembling. The change has come / not once, not once, not once a border here. Everything comes up in this once womb once memory trip. The repetition may be jarring, but these are imbrications in a shingled existence. To write of this occasion does not alleviate the pain or loss.

Your parents live on opposite sides of the war. Water: a boundary between them. Growing up, you could never understand this kind of forgiveness / toward a people who bombed her city day after day. How does she move through war / cross an ocean / land in a new home? It seems you must create a mutable surface on which identity and discourse migrate: that is, identity positions itself within an organism and travels / even when the body is immobile.

The story starts on a night like tonight. Only it doesn't. Because it's morning. Because in reality, it starts eighty-odd years ago: when a mother, who is not a mother but instead a teenager, lives in a city that's bombed / a city on fire. A city [in the only words you can muster] that's slowly dying toward a rebirth. But this isn't the story. This is not a narrative about such things. It is just a sequence of events merging into one. Only they are in another sequence, eternal. Cyclical time skipping beats.

Mama is fourteen when the war starts in Japan. She does not study literature or math or history because all high school students are required to work in a factory. You first hear this story as a child. The radio announces that the factory has been firebombed. On the way home, she meets her father who has heard the news. He's carrying a shovel. What you failed to understand then are the conditions of war. As an adult, your retelling is clinical and condensed. Ojiichan was afraid that he would have to dig her body out of the rubble.

      Ame ame fure fure kaasan ga
      Janome de omukae ureshii na
      Pichi pichi chapu chapu ran ran ran

      Rain rain falling falling Mama
      Brings an umbrella I'm happy
      Splash Splash Splash

      Fire fire bombing bombing Ojiichan
      Brings a shovel Mama's alive
      Boom Boom Boom

No one wants to unbury / bury a child.

This is the story no one has heard. The memory you are unable to write. An erasure of the Tokyo tinderbox / the world forgets to remember. Collective dementia. Devastation in the penumbra.

On March 10, 1945, the US firebombs Tokyo for three hours. Known as the Tōkyōdaikūshū / Great Tokyo Air Raid. Over 100,000 Japanese, primarily civilian women children elderly, are killed / leaving tens of thousands injured & over one million homeless. Often cited as the most destructive single air attack. Ever.

Coincidentally, your parents will marry on this day seven years hence.

Daytime precision attacks on military bases and factories have limited impact / so the US targets children, like Mama, working in them: 銃後の守り手 / Jūgo no mamorite / defenders of the home front.

   銃 gun
   後 back
   銃後 behind the gun
   守り手 guardian
   守り protection
   守 safeguarding
   手 hand [synecdoche for person]

Three hundred B-29 bombers / nearly 2000 tons of incendiary napalm bombs / approximately 16 square miles incinerated / over 250,000 wooden homes and structures burned / temperatures reaching 1800 degrees

The first waves to arrive crisscross the city / attack Koto and Chuo wards. The aircraft that follow trace the kindling / X marks the spot. Gusty winds cause solitary fires. Converge into a conflagration.

charred bodies after singed bodies after scorched bodies across this burnt fire red flame blazing inferno torched paper city

And Mama survives somehow on Tsukishima / 月島 / Moon Island. Some say she's lucky.

And the world erases this atrocity upon her head. The vibration of those burning days / still burning / the heat rising off skin / flamed heart.

Dear Mama. I promise to listen. I promise, Dear Mama. To listen to what you have said. To remember what you have heard. To write what you can't say. Dear Mama. Dear Mama. I promise.

Memory failing is not just the curse of the mother.

The fragile ligatures of an entangled organism. A single cord that stretches through a city perhaps worth knowing. Here in the stark geography of syntax, a forced gift. Unseen debris. A collapse when recalling the selves. That you failed her / failed to tell her story. Unkempt bridges / everywhere / all at once. When another logic in tempo settles into tenebrosity over time. The sentimental years follow an occasional dialogue. What lies ahead? Forgotten burns. Smoke inhalation. Tags and scars. Sudden relief. A stack of postcards that amass grief: *how terrible orange is / and life.* The endurance of words written into scenes, where memory is held. This patchwork / of membranes.

Out of memory—

Mama has told this story many times, but in this retelling she says: *This was not a big bomb, only one block of people dead. The smell of burning people is terrible.*

Blackened earth. What the land tells us about war: *Trees not gonna grow for a long time,* Mama says. The cityscape remembers this trauma.

I forget so easy. So far away. Not Japan, but these memories being pulled by a magnetic force. *If the event has a terminus, it also has a path.* The urgency felt is all for naught. Lost is the spark that ignites the mind. This failure to carry river water home. Slipping through these fingers.

Her words. Thin vellum / proximity pending.

Hanabi / 花火 flowers spark countless fires. There are days when Mama's lucid. There are days when smoke lingers in explosive air. Beauty façade / tragic cortex.

I was fourteen years old when the war started. No food. No clothes. We lucky Tsukishima not bombed. Fukagawa right near Richan's cemetery. Next I went there. I could not find her. All the... I saw so many dead people. Underground. We can hear the bururururu. Planes. Fire bomb. Little can and drop. They dropped inside the underground. Smell. Dead people smell. I couldn't eat because of the smell. People dead is terrible. I saw a lot. Dig in the dirt and make a house. But some bomb hit that place and kill all the people. War is terrible.

A sister lost in smoke becomes a sister lost to womb. *Memory is a future tense.*

In 1945, LeMay targets Fukagawa and other Shitamachi wards, where working-class people and artisans live. A couple hundred years earlier, Bashō's frog splashes in the Sumida River. Once peaceful, now on fire. Years later, Americans use B-29 Superfortress sound effects for sleeping. One person's terror is another's white noise.

What starts with a shovel ends in the Tōkyōdaikūshū. Blended memories. But you don't understand this until now / decades later when you can no longer ask questions. Cloudy vessel. A city bombed for nine months / both before and after the nuclear attacks / turns into one long assault. This firestorm that is never quite extinguished.

Mama watches *Nippon no Uta* / her Japanese songs. She claps her hands. Giggles. Even after the devastation of surviving a war, she is genki / spirited. *Music is best for me / that's why I teach Shigin.*

Her voice a salve. This memory'd salvation.

Mama's younger siblings are evacuated during the air raids. They live in Ibaraki prefecture with Obaachan's family. Ojiichan sweeps ashes off the roof so the house won't catch fire.

Shhe shhe shhe / fire coming out.

Another composed copper sky. Memories erode. The slippage in landslide. There was a time when you knew nothing of Tōkyōdaikūshū. A foreign word / a world away. And now it is. And now its aftermath a living sculpture. The days go by and recall functions as it does. The pain of yesterday replaced by the pain of today. Every continent an appendage known only to itself.

Memorī is all one body. Her stories embedded in you. Some emblazoned on the heart. Some stitched / a scar's thread. The way time warps this memory'd body. But are these stories yours to tell? They would die were it not for the etched seam. Some memories have already vanished. The black hole of minds.

You have too much and not enough information simultaneously. You document one story several times with slight variations. And you have very few details about other attacks. The precarity in memory'd ghosts & other frequencies. Moments of amplification / moments of silence / in these disclosures.

In high school, I had to help Japanese company. We stayed in dormitory. To make some kind of things. We didn't study. They dropped the bomb. And I burned a little but not too bad. Ojiichan and Obaachan heard the news. So they thought I was dead. Just dropped fire. But not big bomb—maybe one block people all dead. Tiny little bomb so fire coming out. Shhe shhe shhe / fire coming out. So maybe we better go home. We don't have bus so I walk. Ojiichan and next door neighbor come with a shovel. I saw the war myself. Lose everything. Make people mean too. I remember how mean people are.

You forget she burns / that she lives away from her family. Sending stars back in time to light the way home.

The sound of sleep / her song's refrain in dreams. The silk century palm. There are days when a string of words is nothing but a false sentence. There are days when a line rebuilds the body / circles past trauma / that simply holds a life.

Shhe shhe shhe / fire coming out.

And we have to help some Japanese factory. So we didn't study. We helped some company make boat outside metal and inside metal. Make insulation. Ishikawajima no company. Bad for the body. Even teacher. Every night they bomb Tokyo. Good thing Tsukishima didn't burn. Drop bomb on company. Burn up company. When I was at the company. Bell ring. Come outside. Because of fire. They drop fire bomb. We come out and try to stop fire. American people know that. Ojiichan heard the news so he bring a shovel, "I better go look for Michiko." Teacher said we better go home. No bus so we had to walk and I saw Ojiichan. He thought I was dead.

Insulation is probably your word not hers. Notes unclear. This shield in isolation. A protective screen.

And the body remembers these acts / decay that is held within. A glow that lights the edge of skin. Echo is a form of time. Sacrifice.

The past a hallowed ground.

Few days later, we found out about the atomic bomb.

And each memory'd spectrum withers in the late season. Dim soon.

Japan lost war yo ne. Now I forget so easy.

Memory is living / this living memory. A slip knot pulled to release. Beyond wishes. Beyond the language caught in the mouth. Tongue swept the teeth of ruins. Syllabary light the way. This moving memorī / looping in and spilling out. Even errors in recall reflect a certain kind of life. Where daily glimpses trill. A horizontal thought above our heads like birds in flight. Margins wrinkle. Messages in transit airs. The migration home.

The past resides in the present and the future too. Each moment circling on itself. Cradling time.

Should this moment die / it dies a star's death. A supernova burst of light. Belonging to tomorrow.

Dear Mama. I promise to listen to what you have said. To remember what you have seen. To write what you can no longer say. Dear Mama. Dear Mama. I promise.

Offerings

This tapestry is woven from imperfect threads—memories worn thin by time, loss, dementia, fluid family mythologies. Inherent in the nature of memory.

Much appreciation to Mama / Sensei Michiko Masuda Pierce for teaching me how to live in this world and for entrusting these memories with me—I love you forever. Special gratitude to my love, Chris Pusateri, for our Saturday morning poetry dates and for taking care of Mama and me all these years. Thankful for Ross M. Pierce II for being the family genealogist and digitally archiving our family photos, Robert H. Pierce and Mayumi (Masuda) Makishima for sharing stories about Ojiichan & Obaachan and the war, and Kerri Lynn (Pierce) Leyba for your daily love & support. This poem is dedicated to Mama, the Masuda / Sakai family, and the people of Tokyo / 東京の人々 who endured this suffering.

Grateful to Veronica Corpuz for writing with me every day for a lunar month in the midst of recovery—much love. Indebted to the Pillowbook Collective for our Sunday murmurations, giving my writing flight. Thanks to K. Blasco Solér, Ali Meyung, Amy Bobeda, Yasamin Ghiasi, JoAnn Balingit, Jill Darling, Esther Lopez, Laura Wetherington, Charlotte Sachs for their friendship, guidance, and notes on this poem. Many thanks to Gabrielle Civil, Mariko Nagai, and Cynthia Arrieu-King for their thoughtful remarks, Liana Martina Maneese for the author's photo, and HR Hegnauer for designing this beautiful cover. Appreciate Sara Veglahn for being an incredible manuscript coach!

And to Eileen Myles—thank you so much for suggesting *MAMA* as the title for this tenderhearted work.

Notes

- Cover photo: Michiko Masuda Pierce, circa 1948, age 20.
- *MAMA* is an excerpt from *Sutured Memorī*.
- Excerpt from "あめふり / Amefuri / Rainy Day"—lyrics written by Hakushū Kitahara, music composed by Shinpei Nakayama (1925).
- *All this and not resembling* is a play on a line from Gertrude Stein's *Tender Buttons*.
- *Memory is a future tense.*—Serena Chopra
- *How terrible orange is / and life.*—Frank O'Hara
- *If the event has a terminus, it also has a path.*—Giles Goodland
- *Moon Island Memorī* is a stitched map of firebombed Tokyo after the Tōkyōdaikūshū in 1945. Medium: Textile—Embroidered Photograph on Cotton. Dimensions: 14 x 8 in.

Historical Record of Tōkyōdaikūshū

- *Probably more persons lost their lives by fire at Tokyo in a six-hour period than at any time in the history of man.*
 —United States Strategic Bombing Survey
- *The human toll that night exceeded that of the atomic bombings of Hiroshima and Nagasaki later that year, where the initial blasts killed about 70,000 people and 46,000 people respectively.*
 —US Department of Energy
- *B-29 raids from those islands began on 17 November 1944, and lasted until 15 August 1945, the day Japan capitulated. The Operation Meetinghouse air raid of 9–10 March 1945 was later estimated to be the single most destructive bombing raid in history.*
 —http://www.onethousandpapercranes.org/iManzanarHistory

Michelle Naka Pierce, born on the summer solstice (her Obaachan's birthday), writes where memory ruptures. Her poetics is shaped by the wandering brush of Zuihitsu and her devoted care for her mother. Both are embodied in her most recent work *Sutured Memori*, which stitches together the matrilineal bodies of mother, grandmother, and daughter—held in a constellation of intergenerational trauma and its aftermath. *MAMA*, excerpted from this collection, is a poem thirty years in the making that honors her mother's resilience and survival of the war.

Author of five full-length books and numerous chapbooks, Pierce embraces collaborative writing 氣 / KI / energies. *Continuous Frieze Bordering Red*, awarded Fordham University Press's Poets Out Loud Editor's Prize, meditates on Rothko's Seagram Murals to document the migratory patterns of an Other, as she travels between countries, languages, seasons, and shifting identities. *She, A Blueprint*, with art by Sue Hammond West (BlazeVox), takes inspiration from Gordon Matta-Clark's "building cuttings" and explores the liminal space in architecture and the body. Finally, *Quarter Light*, written with K. Blasco Solér, Amy Bobeda, and Ali Meyung (Wisdom Body Collective), is a seasonal ritual marking the declining light from autumnal equinox to winter solstice.

Pierce has taught at Naropa University for 25 years; she served as the inaugural dean of the Jack Kerouac School of Disembodied Poetics and director of the Writing Center. Her pedagogy is informed by contemplative and somatic writing practices (such as Akai Ito, Jo Ha Kyu, and intention setting), as well as her background in dance and ekphrastic poetics, where practice-based research meets the mindbody as a site of experimental failure. That is, her teaching emphasizes risk-taking and engaging with language as a living, evolving medium—what the Japanese express as 七転び八起き / Nana Korobi Ya Oki / Fall Down Seven Stand Up Eight.

Born in Tokyo and raised in Albuquerque, Pierce currently resides in the Boulder–Denver metro area with poet Chris Pusateri and Shigin Sensei Michiko Masuda Pierce.

www.ingramcontent.com/pod-product-compliance
Lightning Source LLC
Chambersburg PA
CBHW040307170426
43194CB00022B/2936